Special thanks to Dan Glenn and the team at the Alligator and Wildlife Discovery Center, Madeira Beach, Florida for their knowledge and expertise in all things alligators!

ISBN: 978-1-989506-49-3

© 2021 Lacey L. Bakker
All rights reserved. No parts of this publication may be reproduced or transmitted in any form or by any means, electronically or mechanically, including photocopying recording, or any information storage or retrieval system without either prior permission of the author.
Published in the United States by Pandamonium Publishing House™.
www.pandamoniumpublishing.com

Design: Alex Goubar
Cover Design: Alex Goubar
alexgoubar.com

Grandma Gator's Fascinating Facts

"Come gather round, **hatchlings**; I have a story to tell about the day you were born."

The old gator settled in at the edge of the swamp, and the baby alligators nestled close together to listen to the tale.

"It was a beautifully warm day, and there was not a cloud in the sky. You were merely an egg waiting to hatch as your mothers stood guard. When the day came that you finally arrived, danger **lurked** from above."

"What kind of danger, grandmother?"

"Birds of prey, my dear. A bald eagle had his eyes on you and was ready to swoop in and snatch you, but your mothers acted quickly! You crawled into the protection of their mouths, and they swam and brought you to safety to where we are today."

"But why would an eagle want to hurt us?" a hatchling interrupted.

"Because you look like dinner to them! Some hatchlings were injured in the process of escape and could not be saved. Others relied on humans to help them."

"Humans?"

"Yes, some hatchlings are not as fortunate as you are. They are rescued from farms or from people who should not have them as pets."

"Where do they go?"

"They go to wildlife centers where they are given food, care, and all of the **provisions** that they need to grow strong."

"Will we ever see them again?"

"Most cannot be released into the wild."

"Grandmother, continue the story."

"Predators on the ground were also a threat to your **survival** as hatchlings; large snakes such as pythons, raccoons, opossums, and bobcats were around every corner. So, your mothers' set up a nursery where they would take turns watching and protecting all of you."

"Did you know the markings on your back help your mother identify you? It's similar to a fingerprint where each one is unique, and no two are the same. These markings fade and disappear as you get older to help you blend into your surroundings."

"Wow! What else is special about us?"

"Well, many things! Your bodies are made up of almost all muscle, and you can go for almost two years without eating when you are fully grown!"

"But I'm hungry now!"

"Yes, my dear; your mothers are preparing dinner."

"Tell us more, grandmother!"

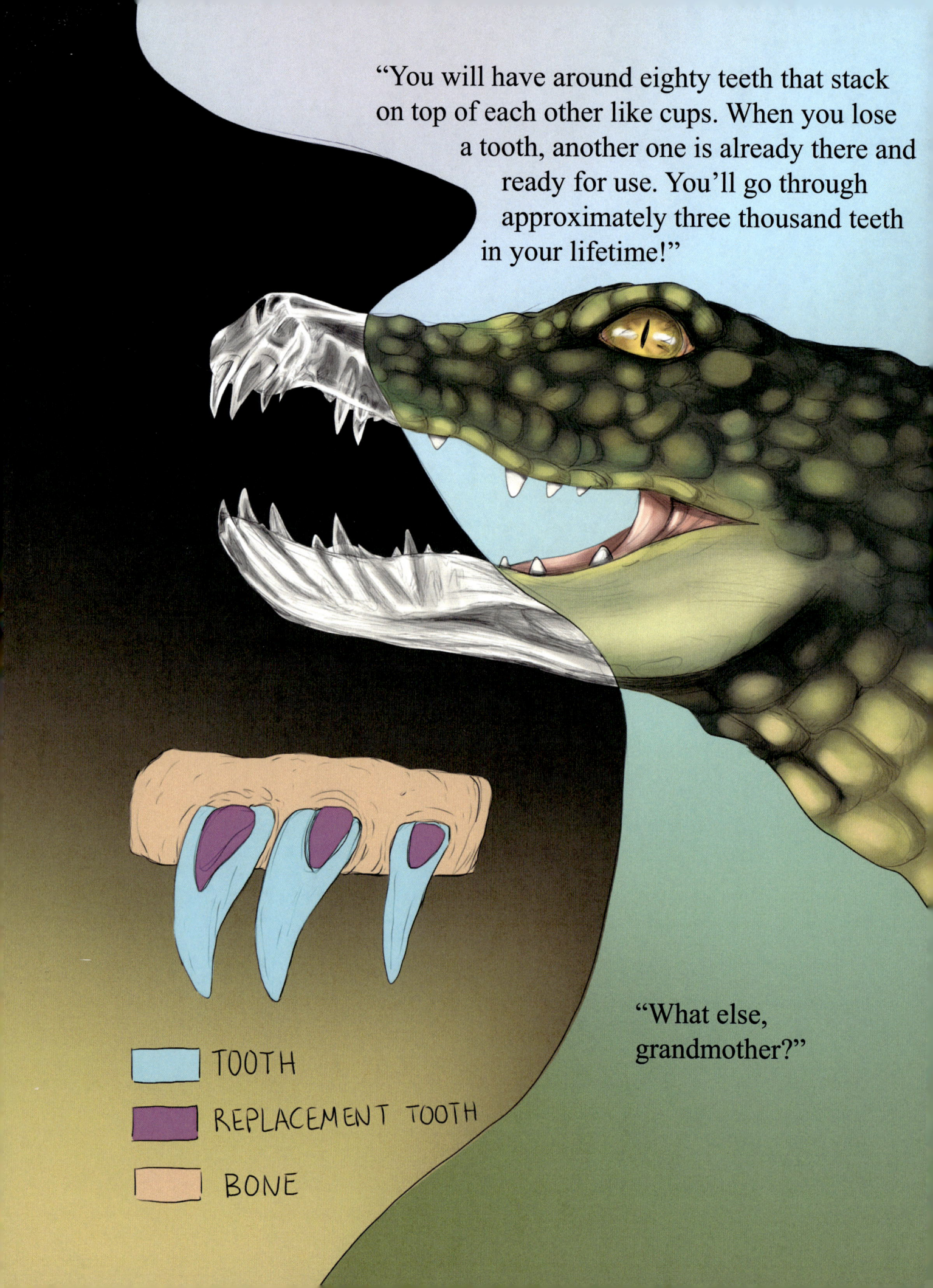

"You will have around eighty teeth that stack on top of each other like cups. When you lose a tooth, another one is already there and ready for use. You'll go through approximately three thousand teeth in your lifetime!"

"What else, grandmother?"

TOOTH

REPLACEMENT TOOTH

BONE

"You've got a very strong jaw. As babies, like you are now, your jaw is as strong as a large dog's. But as you mature, you have a **bite force** that is three times stronger than a lion's! And your cousin, the Nile crocodile, has such as powerful jaw that it is five times more powerful than a great white shark!"

"Whoa! That's awesome!"

"You have dots along your jawline that are pressure sensors."

"What does that mean?"

"It means that because of these special dots, you can **detect** movement from up to 250 feet away! That's as long as two football fields."

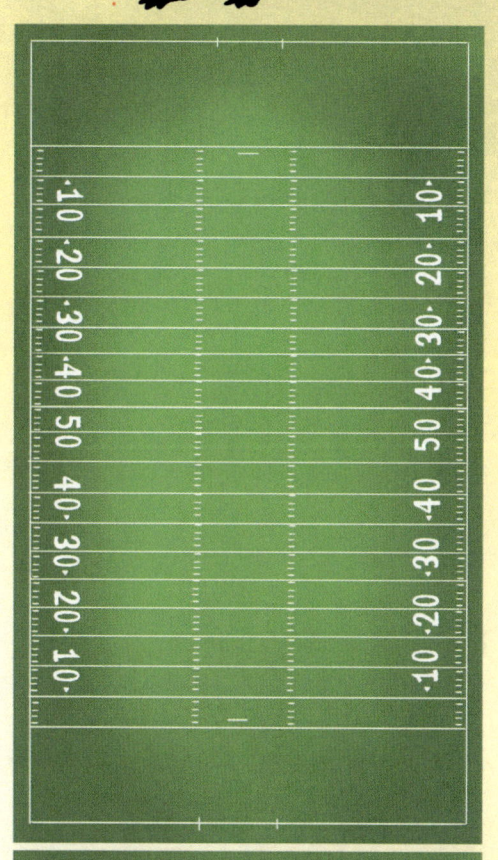

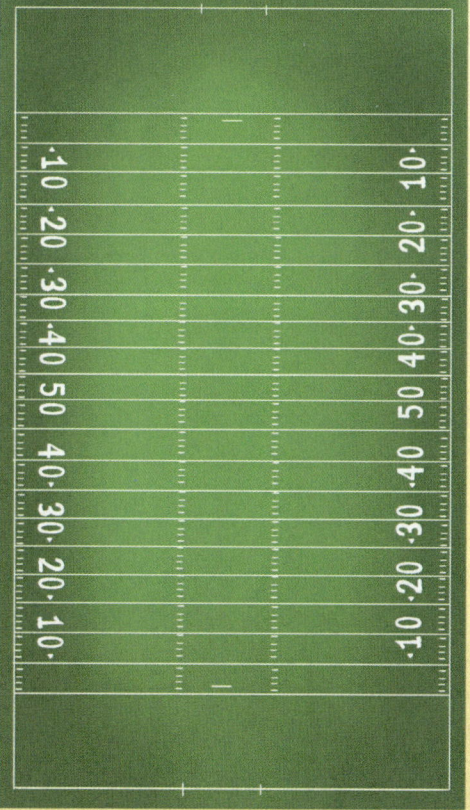

"Wow! Can we run as fast as a football player?"

"I'm not sure, my child, but I do know that we can reach speeds of ten miles per hour on land and twenty miles per hour while swimming. Plus, you can jump almost half your height **vertically** and forwards!"